I never aske

Skills for all who work with reluctant service users...

...social carers: residential, informal and home-based, volunteers, statutory social workers, mental health workers, doctors, nurses, prison staff, police, medical staff

Maggie Kindred - author   *Cath Kindred - illustrator*

4M Publications
10 Station Rd, Southwell, Notts. NG25 0ET
Tel/Ans/Fax: 01636 812883

ISBN: 0 9530494 86

Published by Lulu.com for 4M Publications

Acknowledgments

To all clients and colleagues with great affection and respect. This book exists only because of their contribution.

To partner Michael, for all his wonderful 'behind the page' support, and for laughing at the humorous bits.

To daughter Cath for her creativity and scientific outlook, which have been so valuable.

To social workers Jennifer Fox and Janet Scott for their honest feedback.

To Nigel Horner for his gifted teaching, which has enhanced my own practice.

Of related interest

Developing teamwork
- how to make your team life more satisfying and effective

Once upon a team exercises
- a whole DIY teamwork course in one book

So, you`re on a committee now
- essential committee skills in light-hearted style

Communicating with the public
- all front line workers should have this

Once upon a group
- our original best seller for all groups

Once upon a group exercises
- a course within a single book

For further details visit: www.4mpublications.co.uk

Contents

Social work is not necessarily sociability...

...sometimes it is quite the opposite

This book has grown out of my experience in working with people who have been forced onto the books of social work agencies either because of infirmity or the direction of the courts. 'Social work' has been broadly defined here as all efforts to help people outside your family who are thought by others to be in some sort of need - it is therefore as relevant to informal carers as to probation and child protection officers, and includes all workers who try to make relationships with people who do not want help. I have chosen to call the service users 'clients' even though it is a rather formal word; in my opinion it is the most respectful way to describe receivers of services.

A further word about 'clients': I believe that we are not 'friends' to anyone whom we are helping, either in a professional context, or in a situation which has similar characteristics, eg being a carer for someone who is not a member of your family, and whom you have met through an organisation which exists to respond to needs such as theirs. Blurring the distinction between friendship and this other kind of help usually leads to misunderstanding, and can do actual harm. However a whole range of new possibilities and challenges emerges when you undertake such special work, because it is not 'loaded' with the highly charged emotions which can develop in your personal or family relationships. One well respected expert, Egan (1994), called it 'skilled helping' because most of us find that training is useful in dealing with the challenges and possibilities - hence books like this!

A dedication must go to involuntary clients because I have found, paradoxically, that these service users are the most challenging and rewarding to work with. I feel sorry that involuntary clients are often disliked and sometimes feared, and hope that my positive experiences and reading may be worth sharing with others.

There are many textbooks about the helping process, but few which promote a light-hearted and easily digested approach to the subject matter. The issues faced by clients and workers are far from 'light': they are sad, painful, dangerous and taxing. However I have found that letting fun and learning go hand in hand succeeds better than formal textbooks. The adage is: take people and issues seriously, but not yourself!

It is equally important to acknowledge the contribution of experts to the helping process. I cannot thank certain theorists enough. So my work with students has always been a passionate struggle to promote theory and put it into practice. This book therefore references some of the foundations on which my own practice is built. To this end there will be at least one reference and/or exercise per section, particularly important when I allude to things outside my own experience. The exercises may help you to feel more 'grounded'. They are all well tested and simple to use.

Additionally, because the Internet has made such an important contribution to our ways of finding out things, the book will direct you to sites which give far more detail than could ever be brought into this small volume. Of course these sites may be unavailable or out of date when you need them, but their keywords will point you to others. On this topic, check that material on the web is well researched: you can do this in two ways: a) by checking the flavour and number of sources which have been used, and b) by comparing what several other experts have said on the same subject. This is the approach I have used myself, on the assumption that readers are busy people who would welcome a little spadework done for them.

I am a white, able bodied, heterosexual woman so the book obviously reflects these views of the world. From time to time I will try to highlight areas where it is particularly important to recognise that other perspectives may be totally different from the ones we have taken for granted, particularly in matters of age, disability, class, race, gender and sexuality.

Following on from this: the illustrations are deliberately designed to avoid caricatures. The basic figures therefore represent men, women and children without embellishment.

I am conscious of the number of paradoxes and apparent contradictions in the book. These may irritate you and point up the imprecise nature of 'people work'. Alternatively, you may see this as part of the interest and fascination of such activity - we can never take anyone or anything for granted, and need to be learning every single day of our lives. Certainly, people who do not want services need you to be especially flexible and sensitive - many social customs and conventions have to be re-examined. However I am not setting myself up as an expert; instead hoping to invite debate about all the issues. Following on from this: please excuse any mistakes: proofreading and otherwise.

Some of the issues in the book are common to working with people generally. If a few of these seem obvious, ask yourself why they are not taken seriously more often!

Finally, I wish to acknowledge that my interest in reluctant clients springs as much from my own fierce independence, and sense of inadequacy as a human being, as from any grand principle. I do not find it difficult to understand why people do bad things, or refuse to accept help.

Making a date with someone is not as simple as it seems...

...your good intentions may not be well received

How do you make contact with someone - by email (with the future in mind as more and more people use computers), letter, phone or personal meeting?

It is worth spending a little time on this topic, as the quality of your first approach may win or lose you the battle to speak to someone who does not actually want you. Even if you are based in the same building where your client lives, the same principles apply.

A well known authority, Albert Mehrabian (1972), suggests that 7% of our communication comes through the words we say, 38% through the way we say them, and 55% through our facial expression.

Email has widened our repertoire, and has a number of its own strengths and weaknesses:

- it is quick, easy, and requires less effort for the recipient than replying to a letter

- the growth of the chat room as a method for people to support each other shows that some people feel comfortable with this kind of contact.

However, researchers at Curtin University of Technology have pointed out a few hazards, which are unique to this form of written communication. They discourage the use of **bold**, CAPITALS, and colours, which literally shout at people from the screen. On the positive side, it is worth consulting their site to learn some useful informal devices such as 'smiley' : -). I feel that email has helpfully done away with some of the stuffier conventions of formal letters, but respect must always be the guiding principle.

A letter to someone may be effective because it is not 'loaded' with appearances, but it is obviously very impersonal. Often professional people are surprised and affronted when there is no response to their carefully constructed letter. However if

Mehrabian is somewhere near right, that our letter has only communicated 7% of what we want to get over, which is to be welcoming and friendly, our reluctant client is far more likely to put the letter in the bin than to respond to it.

The telephone allows us to convey warmth in our voice, to respond helpfully to the client's response to our call, and to forge some kind of bond through conversation. However, we are lacking over half our tools for establishing rapport - our facial expressions - on the telephone. No doubt this will change in centuries to come if the online camera becomes as common as the phone is today!

You may conclude that the personal meeting is by far the most effective for first contacts. However it is good to remember that an unannounced call is generally discourteous, and only justified in conditions of extreme emergency, danger, or actual need to apprehend someone who may abscond. The vast majority of situations do not fall into these categories, so the phone or letter will usually have had to be risked first. My experience is that it is amazing how many potential clients will give the new visitor a chance even if they are very suspicious of 'help', sometimes with very good reason.

If you put pressure on people to see you when it is most convenient for your schedule, poor results may follow. There is a very real difficulty here in these days of services under pressure. Juggling all sorts of responses, you simply do not have the flexibility you would like. For me this has meant evening visits when I would have preferred to be doing something else, as it is particularly important for clients who have managed to find work to be fully supported by not having to take time off. Many involuntary clients are of course 'captive' during the day - this makes life a little easier for helpers!

There are other considerations too, some of which may not be so obvious. In my first years of working, I wish I had been aware of many stumbling blocks based around race and culture, over which I fell and hurt both myself and my clients, without understanding why. If I had had access to Keats (2000), for example, I might have known that, in many cultures it is less than acceptable:

- to send a woman to interview a man

- to send a man to interview a woman

- to interview a married woman alone, or without her husband being present

- to send a person of one religion to interview a person of a different religion when there is conflict between the two religious groups

- to mention the name of people who have recently died

- to look directly into a person's face when speaking

- to cause the listener to lose face

Obviously these examples do not apply to everyone whose racial background is not western, as there is enormous variety according to local custom. Where individuals have spent the majority of their lives also affects their practices, and people may operate in different ways at different ages. You and your client do not necessarily have a choice about working together, nor about the content of the discussion. However, it makes all the difference in the world if you know you are having to act offensively. First of all you may be able to make significant changes such as taking someone with you with whom your client will feel comfortable. If this is not possible you can convey to him/her that you are sorry that a more appropriate person is not available, and that you need to raise very difficult matters. You will never be in a position to respond accurately to all members of different races or social classes, nor be completely accepted as one of their own, but you can show sensitivity by recognising that there are very different interpretations of even the simplest gesture or word.

The more you can communicate sincerely to people that you understand their reservations about seeing you, the better your success rate is likely to be. It gets easier:

'Don't introduce me to that man! I want to go on hating him, and I can't hate a man whom I know' Charles Lamb (1775-1834).

Sending messages...

...not the ones you thought, though

Actually this is about what begins to happen even before you say hello. Although closely related to non-verbal communication, it is much less easy to define, but is important enough to deserve a mention on its own.

When we meet someone, a large number of impressions take root in each of us faster than the speed of light, and certainly before we have said hello. An example would be the fleeting thoughts you may have when you see what kind of car a visitor has just parked outside your house. A student once described my whole lifestyle on the basis that I drove a Ford Fiesta! Making a judgement about someone's smart or otherwise car is possibly easily recognised, but I believe that there are dozens of small but significant decisions made inside each of us about other people all the time, of which we are not even aware. These judgements, or assumptions is probably a better word, can be absolutely lethal, because they bring with them a small, unseen label which says bad or good.

Your reluctant client may have had bad experiences with professionals. So all your efforts to be friendly and present yourself helpfully are played against this background, even if the client greets you politely. You can take it for granted, I believe, that a huge number of negative assumptions are being made about you, and that these will not be easily shifted. It helps to be comfortable with this, and not to try to prove yourself. The gaining of trust may only happen over time and then only partially. Be prepared for never coming over as the concerned, honest person you really are.

Try the following, which will make the above points much more clearly than going into further explanations:

You need either to do this one with a small group of colleagues whom you don't know well, or a group of friends who can be relied on to be honest. People you don't know come closer to replicating a meeting with a new client, but also expect some surprises from people who know you well. You will need a big piece of paper and felt pen. It would be helpful for a group member to agree to write notes on the paper for you.

1. Explain to the group that you are going to ask them to make guesses about things they don't know about you, using facts they do know. These need to be things you can answer yes or no to, not guesses about your feelings or personal qualities, as these can vary from day to day, or may be subjective. Example: 'I think you are teetotal since I've never seen you drink alcohol.'

2. Ask your helper to write each example on the piece of paper but don't give the answers until everyone has finished guessing.

3. Now give an honest yes or no to each guess.

4. Next comes the risky bit: ask the contributor of each statement what their guess, or assumption, about you made them feel towards you. Example: "When I said I thought you were a teetotaller, in my heart of hearts I think teetotallers are a bit goody-goody."

5. Discuss the accuracy or otherwise of people's assumptions, and the sort of evidence they had for them.

Comment: I am willing to bet that there were a few surprises all round. We are always finding out things about people, even if we make a career of it!

'You can live a lifetime, and at the end of it, know more about other people than you know about yourself' Beryl Markham (1902-1986) - first woman to fly solo across the Atlantic.

Staying safe...

... a topic which needs some attention

'Deeds of violence in our society are performed largely by those trying to establish their self-esteem, to defend their self-image, and to demonstrate that they, too, are significant' (May 1972, pp. 21-3).

Many involuntary clients are thus described, so the need for personal safety must be faced squarely. I wish to strike a balance between over-emphasising danger and pretending that some clients do not have the potential for harm. Here are some thoughts which have been drawn from both my own experience and that of others.

You do need to know if the person you are going to meet has any history of violence. Some people, particularly informal carers, do not like to know about someone's past, as they do not wish to form judgements. It may be useful to unpick this a little: while it is quite true that clients often feel they have been pre-judged, many are reassured by your awareness of how they have come to be in their current position. It can be much more embarrassing and difficult, even tedious, for the client to have to tell the whole story again, as they see it, to you. You can only decide about whether someone is safe to be seen on the basis of information, not principles about labelling people. This is not an area for you to take risks - there are plenty of others where you can. Reluctant clients do include people who have the kind of symptoms which result in unpredictable behaviour, who are desperately angry that you have been forced on them, or who are out of control through alcohol or drugs.

Before visiting you need to make a risk assessment. This could be formalised by your agency: if so you will have some form filling to do. If you find this a tedious waste of time, it is worth remembering that such procedures grew out of tragedies which happened partly because there were no safety nets.

Being safe also applies to keeping yourself away from situations which make you vulnerable to accusation, be it sexual abuse, fraud, unethical conduct, or neglect. It follows that all kinds of 'playing at being friends' are no-go areas. Having coffee with someone in a public, therefore relatively safe, environment, where the purpose is very definitely to talk over the thing you are meeting about, can be very helpful; an intimate dinner for two 'after work' is definitely not.

When you meet your client it is vital is to ask how the person sees things *now*. What they tell you will give you some pointers as to how far or near they seem from other people's perceptions of them. It is usually impossible to negotiate with someone drunk or drugged. If you suspect any life threatening behaviour or condition, get help quickly.

Then there is your response to cues: I remember being taught how important it is to respond quickly when acting in a play, otherwise the scene goes completely flat. In skilled helping your response needs to be so fast at times as to be instantaneous, when anticipating someone's mood or illness level. It is also worth noting that silence, which is often so valuable in counselling, can be very intimidating for some fearful clients, and is best avoided as a technique for helping such people to open up.

Knowing that the same cue has different meanings according to your cultural roots is really crucial here. For example, I, a British woman, was brought up to understand that 'not looking someone in the eye' is either devious or rude. My female contemporaries, whose family roots may be in Eastern cultures, may well lower their eyes out of modesty or deference, particularly if they are speaking to a man. For detailed help on this subject see on the web: *A world of gestures (Archer 1992),* which includes some fun exercises for you to try.

My experience is that horror and violent films definitely affect some people with mental health problems, because the latter have high sensitivity. This is worth considering if you are watching television with your client.

If in any doubt, take someone with you, leave if you are scared, and keep well out of arms' reach. You are within your legal rights to carry a personal alarm, pepper pot or aerosol such as deodorant, but not a lethal weapon.

Think about what you wear: for example scarves and long earrings can be grabbed.

In all cases, not just risky contacts, colleagues should know where you are at all times, and when they expect to hear from you again.

You may not have total control over the scene of meeting if you are in someone's home. This presents another potentially hazardous area - kitchens with their knives are dangerous.

Finally, in my experience, more assaults have happened in unexpected situations such as being accosted in the corridor of a hostel by a complete stranger, with your own client innocently in his own room. The moral of this has to be: always maintain an appropriate wariness - it will not detract from being warm and friendly.

This is an area where some expert advice could be helpful: try *Personal safety at work: a guide for everyone,* which is produced by the Suzy Lamplugh Trust, and includes case studies which will ring true for most people.

How you look does matter ...

...for whom are you dressing?

Many people would say that we have to dress for our clients. This is one of the world's obvious statements which needs unpicking: I am a conventional looking elderly woman - should I try to make myself look like a teenager in order to establish rapport with one? If we were to take this road it would be difficult to see how anyone would make contact with all the people different from her/himself seen in a day: this includes race, age, sexual orientation, class and disability. On the other hand, it does seem to be important to make your choice of clothes according to your public appearances for the day.

Wearing conspicuously expensive looking clothes is unlikely to endear you to a poor person. On the other hand, 'dressing down' is insulting. Formal occasions such as court require you to discard your more casual wear, however boring this may seem, if you are to attain the best result for your client. Both men and women need to think about whether their clothes are sexually provocative. It is notable that psychotherapists' collective experience has led them to furnish both their persons and their rooms in a warm, welcoming but non-controversial way. Individuality is best expressed through your responses to people, and fortunately the points we have been making about your facial expression and attitude are much more important.

I am very well aware that you may disagree with aspects of the above. In 40 years of experience I have never known a group of professionals reach complete agreement on a dress code! However there does seem to be some accord on the starting principle: dress for your client not for you. Try this one for fun:

1. Ask members of a group of friends or colleagues how they chose the clothes they are wearing today.

2. In the responses, note how far people have consciously dressed

a) to please the people they are going to meet,
b) to please themselves, which includes activities

24

they are going on to after the group they are in now.

3. Note the differences between men and women on this topic.

4. See if you can come to any conclusions as a group which affect the way you each dress tomorrow.

Obviously it is not within the spirit of this book for judgemental comments to be made about other people's apparel. Rather, it is interesting to notice points coming up which you or others may not have thought about.

Interesting site*: www.kevinhogan.com/nonverbal-communication-body-language.htm*

What do you do after you have said hello...

...make a contract!

As helpers, we can be our own worst enemies. In order to try to be friendly, un-intimidating and informal, we sometimes leave our clients nonplussed about our purpose. Howe (1990), on the basis of his research, said that clients felt confused, baffled and irritated by social workers who did not make their intentions clear. For reluctant clients, add a big element of fear of our intentions.

What helps is to ask clients what they imagine we have come for, then state our purpose in as few words as possible. If we are there to supervise, it is much better to be honest than to pretend we have just dropped in. Next it is useful to agree on how the meetings will go, how long they will normally last, and what the client hopes to gain from them. A negative or angry answer to the last is to be expected, but it is important as a chance to ask what *could* help. For example, a young man who could not leave his house was asked if there was anything at all which would make it easier for him to get out. His reply was quite simple: 'Try after dark'. Fortunately this conversation happened to take place in the winter! However the worker wanted the young man to succeed so much she would have been prepared to take him out at 11pm at midsummer. There is a solution to most things!

What definitely does not work is for the helper to decide the aims without consultation with the client. But, I hear you saying, isn't that precisely what work with involuntary clients is all about: forcing things on people who do not want them? My experience is that the 'force' element is actually very small - simply that you are in contact. The rest is actually much more negotiable and open-ended than this. If it isn't, the client will no doubt be living in a setting which is protective to both him/her and you.

One thing which can make the client feel freer is not to ask hundreds of questions, unless of course that is the precise purpose of your visit, which would have been stated at the beginning. Instead, it is better to observe and listen. If clients feel that you are not going to interrogate them, they are far more likely to open up. As an example, I had a job which required me to do a monitoring visit every fortnight. I found that, rather than go through a tedious routine of asking the client each time how he/she felt, what had been happening, and so forth, it worked to agree from the outset that worker and client would bring items to their meetings which each wished to talk about, and that there would be no 'small talk'. It was surprising sometimes how much the clients put on the agenda - at other times the meeting would last only ten minutes.

It is essential to address the matter of confidentiality at the outset. Many workers are uncomfortable about this, fearing that their relationship with the client will suffer if they tell her/him that their discussions are not confidential. It is certainly the case that there are some agencies whose strength is that they preserve confidentiality whatever is revealed. I cannot help feeling that there must be some dilemmas for such agencies: for example is it really feasible not to pass on knowledge of a murder? As far as involuntary clients are concerned, I feel it is more helpful to say that everything is potentially shared with colleagues, because of the need to work as a team for the service user's benefit.

The ramifications of confidentiality do not end with the client. Workers need to talk to their supervisors: the issues are exactly the same as for client relationships. I remember working with a student who insisted that all supervisory discussions must be confidential - I and he simply had to agree to differ!

I feel that this section also needs to address the *unstated* contracts which can be more powerful than the official ones. As a starter for this, try the following with your colleagues:

Note: This can be an intense exercise, so leave plenty of time for discussion and support.

Explain that all families and teams develop a set of 'rules' which can be very powerful, even though people are often unaware of them and they are certainly not written down! As far as teams are concerned, these are in addition to the formal policies and rules.

Examples:

- *Never sit in the boss's chair in the office*
- *Don't eat at your desk*
- *Always offer to make a cup of coffee for others when making one for yourself*

28

1. As a group, think about life in your team during an ordinary day. Make a list of 'rules' which you think operate in the team.

2. Read out what everyone has written.

3. Think about how each rule came into being, and what, if anything, should be done about each one. Is it reasonable to have some unwritten rules in a team which are accepted and not questioned?

4. Discuss how many of the rules are positive?

Comment:

'House rules' are an inevitable part of group life. Frequently they are useful: for example most people feel uncomfortable if they think they are wrongly dressed for an event. Some people take pleasure in breaking the rules. What definitely causes distress is breaking rules which you did not know existed, a bit like swimming in a clear blue sea which has treacherous undercurrents. On the other hand, rules like bringing cake on someone's birthday are fun and enhance team life.

It may be helpful in understanding all this to refer to Transactional Analysis (Cryer 1990). This theory suggests that all young individuals learn certain ways of feeling and behaving which become habitual when they are older - 'a life -script'. One individual's script is very different from another's because of differences in how they were treated in early life by people they relied on and learned from (Cryer 1990, p. 368). Individuals are seldom aware of their scripts because these scripts are so much part of them that that they do not normally consider examining them, and they might even have difficulty in teasing out what they are. So, house rules generally aim at making individuals more comfortable: sometimes this is at the expense of others. How far do your rules enable people, or do some of them make some members seem more powerful than they really are?

Returning to your agreements with clients: have you or they unwittingly applied a few rules which are getting in the way? This includes things like: 'The previous worker always did it this way.' 'I need a cigarette after one hour'.

Finally, if you hate contracts, it is worth remembering times when you felt in a situation where you did not know what was expected of you - what would have helped?

You may feel yourself to be up against formidable opposition...

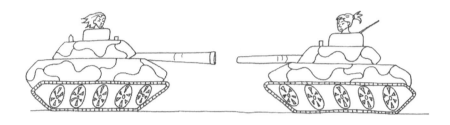

... it is worth remembering that the other person may feel exactly the same

Suppose you are a person who is new to the art of trying to help someone in a professional or caring way (if this is actually the case, well and good, as you will not have got into set patterns). It is normal to feel very nervous, and certainly not that you have a lot of power. One of the paradoxes of this situation is that being forced into accepting help immediately throws the recipient into also feeling powerless, as you will recall when in the dentist's chair, or on the operating table. If someone has been ordered to have assistance, or has a disability which gives them no choice, this feeling of powerlessness is magnified a thousand times. So it is about fifteen all as to who feels the more helpless: helper or receiver. A challenging thought: we are part of our client's problem and we can often be told as much in no uncertain terms! Accepting this unpalatable fact, and letting the other person know that you have, is a big step towards establishing rapport.

It is interesting that, in quite ordinary situations, people who appear to have power are not always the ones you might think. To illustrate this point, try the following:

The power tree *

1. Think of your family, a group of people with whom you work, or a club you belong to.

2. Draw yourself somewhere on the power tree to show how you feel in relation to other people in the family or group, the top part of the tree being the most powerful.

3. Draw the others in the group where you feel they are in relation to you and each other. This may or may not be related to your position in the family or group, eg you could be the eldest in the family or the manager of a team, yet feel yourself to be right at the bottom of the 'pecking order'.

Did you discover any surprises? If so, it may be helpful to start by recognising the fact that all groups, from the highest powered corporation to the most informal of organisations in a small village, depend on the use of power.

Secondly power in itself is not wrong, it is a necessary part of life. A young child cannot have power equal to that of an adult. It is the misuse of power, or oppression, which is unacceptable. This applies to everyone. The person who is low paid but has the key for a particular cupboard is very powerful, and has it within his/her grasp to stop productivity for a day - this makes her/him as powerful as the boss for a time. It is the labels which accompany the power which make people squirm: 'I'm only the secretary', 'He's a manipulator'.

'I sometimes think that 99 per cent of suffering has to do with how devalued people feel by the labels put on them or the derogatory opinions they hold about themselves' (Hoffman 1993, p. 79).

* Substantially reproduced, with permission, from *Once upon a team exercises* © 4M Publications 2001

The space you create may make or break your working relationship ...

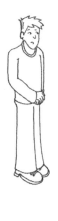

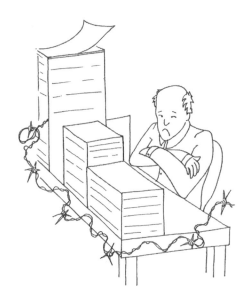

...this is an aspect we cannot take for granted

Most people know that it is helpful not to invade another person's personal space by getting too close to them. However it is useful to remind ourselves that this is different in other cultures. As an example, some Middle Eastern people and Latin Americans stand nearer to each other than westerners in formal contexts (BBC World Service, undated).

There is a contradiction here: you need to be as undefensive as possible, so try not to sit behind a desk, on a higher chair than your client, stand when she/he is sitting, or anything else which can enhance your powerful position. Being undefensive is not the same as being unsafe - it is trying to leave as much control in the hands of your client as you possibly can.

A biologist friend of mine once pointed out that we are much nearer the animal kingdom than we like to think. Perhaps that is why our territory is so important to us - *don't* sit in the boss's chair!

This is an area where you need, and will find interesting, much more detail. Try:

www.sitemaker.umich.edu/356.kyprianides-

Anything you say may be used in evidence...

...this is nearly always true

It is hardly surprising that involuntary clients feel threatened by
workers' and organisations' written records. For a start popular
fiction adds *'against you'* to the legal caution quoted here.
Secondly my experience is that many written records are quite
unbelievably bad in their condemnatory, biased, and inaccurate
way of describing people and events.

This is a shame because written 'evidence' can be a brilliant tool
for helping the reluctant client to feel more confident.

This book therefore seeks to change the *'evidence against you'* to *'evidence for you'.*

One of the problems of written (now read 'computer stored') records is the fact that they were traditionally kept from the client. Following the legislation beginning in 1987, which allowed people much more access to their personal files, record keeping improved slightly, but not as much as the author might have hoped. Sadly, many organisations complied with the letter of the law, but not its spirit, by making access to files a complicated process, and in some cases a service for which you have to pay. For more details of the history of opening up access to files see *Wikipedia,* the free encyclopaedia on the Web.

I believe that records are essential - this is one of the differences between 'skilled helping', as defined, and other kinds of friendship. Where involuntary clients are concerned, you will in any case be expected to produce records for monitoring purposes - health, progress, other people's protection, for example. So here goes to turn *'against you'* into *'for you'.*

I can only remember one client who did not wish to see what was written about her. She felt so desperate about her badness she could not believe that there could be anything good in her file. In the case of most reluctant clients, sharing some aspect of their record is an excellent place to start work. This could be reading together the client's last formal review, or client and worker writing what they think has happened during their current meeting, and sharing the results, even making a formal application to read the back files. Whatever conflict may arise, even if the client disagrees with whatever you or others have written, there are excellent opportunities for helping him/her to underline everything positive there is in the file. Obviously you will consider safety: the client's state of mental health and the nature of what is written being of prime importance. I would like to say that dangerousness in itself is not a reason for withholding information; I have experience of sharing records with some of the most dangerous people in England. Obviously safeguards have to be in place for yourself, other people, and the client after the session, where there is any question of harm ensuing.

There is a very simple guiding principle, which has served me well: never write anything which you would not like to read about yourself. This is as much about the way things are written as the content. It helps your relationship with the client enormously for you to change a word which he/she does not like, for the client to point out a mistake or an omission which has been made - most files provide plenty of scope for this!

However the client cannot have sole charge of the content of the record. You must note everything which seems important to you, however unpleasant. So there could be occasions where you share with the client a general expression of concern, and discuss the record more fully later. For example, if you intend calling in another professional immediately after you have left the client's home, you may need to be less than open if you believe he/she would disappear if you told him/her what you had decided. Of course your relationship will need some repair after this - most people will then acknowledge that care sometimes demands extreme measures.

I believe that everything is ultimately useful in working with your reluctant client. The difficult circumstances just described would be excellent material for future meetings: you can read out your clear and accurate account of exactly how you found him/her to be when in a bad state.

The parts of your records which cannot be shared are those relating to other people: 'third parties'. These could be client's relatives, friends or other clients. Reports from professionals may also be protected in this way, though my experience is that some workers are over-protective; ostensibly for the sake of clients, but it could be that they are guarding themselves! Many agencies have systems in their file sections for keeping such records separate and for labelling them confidential: this is obviously good practice. Clients usually understand other people's rights to confidentiality, especially when you explain that the same rules apply for themselves. In certain cases you may be able to preserve confidentiality in situations where there is unlikely to be any question of legal action as a result of the information. However in writing this I have not been able to think of an example, hence my guiding principle that everything told to you is potentially significant and needs to be shared with your colleagues.

Accuracy is obviously essential: not as easy as it sounds. A useful little exercise is to estimate the percentage of inaccuracy you think there is in eyewitness accounts of events, especially where the situation is emotionally charged (result at bottom of this page). I am willing to bet that the percentage is more than you thought.

If the above has not already raised the same thought for you, I feel that recording is an area in which we definitely need some training. The web offers many free sets of guidelines, and *Social care practice (Miller 1996)* is a useful book.

Finally, I would like to assure you that the only problems I have ever had with sharing records with clients is the judgemental language found in them - mine and other people's!

Malpass (1996) estimated 15% inaccuracy in eyewitness accounts.

What you believe matters...

...maybe more than you think.

It seems important first to describe what I mean by 'believe'.
I am primarily talking about beliefs about people, rather than
which religious group you belong to.

In order to try to avoid this part being rather nebulous in an
otherwise practical book, I have looked at some 'results', a
tricky area when discussing involuntary clients, about whom
I have found extensive pessimism.

One aspect of your helping ability is feeling with or for people - empathy. This sets the background for your work, but it is by no means the whole answer where involuntary clients are concerned. An expert in this field, Trotter (1999), found that when helpers made comments which seemed to excuse the crimes clients had committed, sometimes the re-offending rate went up. Perhaps this revelation is something of a relief, as there will certainly be people you cannot empathise with: murderers and child abusers being examples for many people.

However several researchers have strengthened my conviction that if the helper believes that the client can change for the better, this is more likely to happen - in other words - optimism. Kirk et al (1993) noted the effect that workers' positive attitudes had when they were providing intensive services to clients. The book *Learned Optimism* by Martin Seligman (1995) has almost become a classic in education, describing the way young people 'catch' the mental attitude of the teacher. Very recently Miller and Rollnick (2004) studied interviews between workers and clients in depth, and again the important part worker optimism played was noted in results.

In addition, the comments made elsewhere in this book about clients sensing the true feelings of the worker are reinforced by Trotter, when he noted that when probation officers made negative comments about clients such as 'lazy', 'no-hoper', in file notes, their clients had a higher re-offending rate.

So, as you cannot help your feelings, how can you become a more effective helper of people whose behaviour may arouse in you nothing but disgust?

As with all personal work, there are no cast iron recipes, but my experience is that increased understanding of both yourself and the client can make dramatic changes. This is a complicated matter, as becoming more understanding is not something you can always do at will. Your inability to understand some aspect of others may be deeply embedded in your own experience, or you may simply lack some of the essential pain experience which you can transfer to new situations. However the author believes that feeling yourself into new and uncomfortable positions *can* to some extent be learned. Try the following:

Read the following passage to a friend or colleague at normal speed without practising first.

We know something of the pattern of breakdown of language in Alzheimer's disease. The first change that occurs is in tasks such as naming - that aspect of language that is concerned with the meaning of words (semantic system). Then follows a process of deviation and simplification of grammar (syntax), and then the disordered use of sounds (phonetic breakdown). Word-finding problems become apparent in conversation, and the ability to name things becomes noticeable. As the disease progresses speech becomes increasingly repetitive, with less attention paid to conversational rules, and it appears to be increasingly egocentric. Interestingly, it appears that the ability to read aloud often remains to a relatively late stage, although comprehension of what is read may long since have been eroded (Goldsmith 1996, p.54).

Now repeat back to your helper what you have just read.

This activity gives you a small taste of the daily struggle of the person with dementia in dealing with everyday communication. You may argue that the piece is hardly 'everyday' - but it would be if you are a dementia expert. You may have avoided doing the exercise at all because you are not confident in your reading abilities. If, like me, aged sixty plus, you are aware of the gradual, normal, eroding of ability to retain and reproduce words, you might have felt some anxieties about whether you are, in fact, developing dementia. I believe that it is often necessary to experience a degree of discomfort in order to become more empathic, and someone trustworthy to talk to is absolutely essential. The clients who teach you the most are the ones whom you find hardest: this applies to many involuntary clients if they have committed actions you find difficult to forgive.

Obviously your own specific situation at the time plays a part: if you are a survivor of recent domestic violence you can hardly be expected to believe that that your client's abusive behaviour is going to change. It is also sometimes helpful to avoid certain situations for the time being: for example bereavement counsellors usually advise recently bereaved helpers not to work with people in the same situation for a few months.

This book exists to help us work with involuntary clients, as I think that there are certainly things we can do to change our attitudes and enhance our working practices. However it is worth saying that some people will always be more effective when their clients are there by choice - we are all different!

'She spent her life helping others...

...you could tell the others by the hunted look'

The above quotation is from the late C.S. Lewis, a wise and sensitive observer of human beings. It is very hard for us to remember that genuine helping often involves avoiding finding solutions for people. But, I hear you saying, we are working with involuntary clients - solutions are essential. Very true, but we sometimes give the impression that *everything* is compulsory. Prison is meant to punish by depriving someone of his/her liberty, but provide rehabilitation within the confining walls.

Our 'imprisonment' of involuntary clients is our presence in their lives: once there we are not expected to force feed them. Of course in certain circumstances, treatment programmes are indeed prescribed, such as those for paedophilia. These measures make it possible for clients to return to the community, so motivation tends to be reasonably high.

A large proportion of involuntary clients are those with a physical disability. In recent years groups for people with disability have tried to educate the more able-bodied of us out of our insensitive, well-meaning ways of operating. Test yourself out on the following:

How should you communicate directly with people who may have a disability ?

1. Do you offer help?

2. How do you offer help?

3. What do you do if they say' no thanks'?

4. What should you say if they say '**** off'?

5. Can you say 'Be seeing you' to a blind person without offending them?

6. Can you say 'I hear congratulations are in order' to someone who is deaf, without offending them?

7. Can you say 'Well I'll be running along then' to a person in a wheelchair, without offending them?

8. How do you know what seat or position is best for a person who is disabled?

9. How do you shake hands with someone who is blind?

10. Would you like a stranger to ask these questions of you:
   - How long have you been like this?
   - What's wrong with you?

Or to the person's carer:
   - Does he take sugar?

Answers at end of section.

I would argue that all the questions are appropriate, whatever the situation. Judith Usiskin (1998), from whose expertise in this field this exercise originated, says that a good rule of thumb is to ask the person what they want or need you to do.
A number of examples come from my experience:

- A worker was being interviewed for a job. One of the interview panel members was a wheelchair user. The panel chairperson asked the interviewee to move the person in the wheelchair across the room. The unwary applicant did so without asking the wheelchair user how he would like to proceed. We imagine the applicant was unsuccessful!

- A worker had just finished what he thought was a very thorough assessment of a client's needs, including a range of services, medical help, and home care. The worker's supervisor spoke to the client to check the assessment, and asked him what he thought his needs were. The client replied 'Some sex, some legs, and a car'!

- A student was working in a hostel for young disabled people. The philosophy of the establishment was self-direction at all times. A young service user caused this student to be disconcerted when he asked her to put his woollens in the washer on hot, thereby ruining them.

If I had been the student in the above example, I admit I would have been tempted to put the washer on a more appropriate setting. It would have been better to point out the different wash cycles! To learn by trial and error is the kind of ordinary experience able-bodied people take for granted - those with disability suffer from necessary, but sometimes more disabling, protection. All the situations require choice to be given first, action second.

It seems appropriate to end this section by referring to the guiding principle of the hostel where the above incident took place: 'helping others' means doing only that which clients cannot do themselves, 'being their arms and legs', but not their central nervous system.(Obviously there are a few exceptions to this, but not many).

Answers
1. *Yes.*
2. *Tactfully!*
3. *'That's OK then'.*
4. *'That's OK then'.*
5. *Yes.*
6. *Yes.*
7. *Yes.*
8. *Ask them.*
9. *Ask them if you can shake their hand.*
10. *No!!!*

Have I any rights at all...

...if so, what are they?

Involuntary clients often have a very strong sense of being deprived of their rights. You may feel that some of them have brought this on themselves, and that others are simply unfortunate in being forced to accept help through no fault of their own. All have equal cause to feel aggrieved at your invasion of their lives. It is worth exploring different kinds of 'taking over', with a view to making the process as constructive as possible.

If someone wishes to kill themselves, our society says this is not a decision you can condone in the short-term, whatever your personal view. The strength of organisations such as the Samaritans is in their leaving the client free to make even such an extreme choice, though of course they use every possible resource to try to help the client find life-preserving paths. However this book is primarily for practitioners who are face to face with their clients by law or extreme need, and who have a duty to decide whether someone is a danger to him/herself or others, then to remove that danger, albeit temporarily.

In spite of this, all clients, including reluctant ones, have a substantial number of rights, however extreme their situation, though it is not usually helpful to point this out as a grand theory. The beginnings of a list might go something like this:

- be treated with respect at all times

- be asked to do something before being told to do it

- ask for a second opinion (obviously this may not happen on the spot)

- be consulted wherever possible

- have access to an advocate, translator or representative

- be advised about how to make a complaint

- continue to receive a service

- have access to family life as far as possible - this is where you can help by making every effort to strengthen ties

Some of these rights are embodied in law, notably

49

Your client does not have the right to:

- abuse you verbally in any way at all, but especially on

    grounds of race, gender, sexual orientation, age, disability or social standing

- be violent towards you

- threaten or subject you to emotional pressure

Verbal abuse is a difficult area, and it would be hard to find a consensus about it. I began my career by thinking that clients needed to shout at me, and that letting them do so was a helpful release. Over the years I have come to the position that allowing people to abuse me verbally actually demeans them - they can do without this as they are so demeaned already. So you may agree with me that it is useful to tell the person gently that you do not like what they have just said, or that you won't accept it. Exceptions: if someone is out of touch with reality, either through illness, alcohol or drugs, there is no point in challenging, and it may even be dangerous to do so.

Threatening to withdraw the service is always wrong in the context of involuntary clients, because it is not an option. Perhaps, though, it is right to change the worker if, for example, abuse is based on someone's colour or gender. This also has its negative side, as a change to a white worker from a black one may be seen as colluding with racism. On complex matters such as these the worker's rights to be consulted about such decisions certainly come into the foreground.

You may find it useful to have a look at the following situation:

1. *Imagine you go by appointment to visit Alice, an 80 year old woman whom you know quite well. She is not particularly frail,*

but has recently been in hospital for a routine operation, and you were called in to provide some support on her return home, because she had once had a blackout. She is extremely independent, and has asked you to leave her alone on several occasions. However she is always polite and opens the door to you.

2. When you reach Alice's house, you ring the bell, but there is no answer. You look through the window and see that she is sitting in her usual chair, asleep. However she is slumped in an uncomfortable looking position, almost on the floor. You knock on the window, but fail to rouse her. You go away for half an hour and return. Alice is in exactly the same position, and again does not respond to your knocking.

3. You have 3 alternatives

 - *return later that day*

 - *return another day*

 - *force your way into the house*

 Which do you choose?

I have found that this situation aroused strong feelings when offered to students in training. It goes to the heart of the human rights versus duty to care debate. Whichever way you chose to proceed, you would obviously not do so without consultation. During this you may find the arguments reproduced between senior personnel, the police if you decide to involve them, and friends/colleagues. If you are asked to proceed in a way which seems to you inhuman, such as leaving a situation alone when you think it needs action, it is worth just asking whether you may need saving from yourself. Situations which definitely need prompt action are in one sense the easy ones. 'Alice' could land you before a complaints panel if you invade her home and she objects, or a coroner's court if you decide to leave her and she dies.

My guiding principle, which may be different from yours: better to have someone alive and angry than dead but unviolated.

What many people think of as a problem ...

...is in fact a dangerous opportunity

When I was training, I noticed for the first time how clients in hospital seemed particularly receptive to my efforts to help. This could be explained somewhat negatively by the fact that being ill makes people so low and lacking in resistance that they will do anything you ask, or that the authority structure in a hospital is so intimidating that they dare not protest.

Another, somewhat more optimistic way of thinking, is the idea that being in hospital is always a crisis. Our society usually uses the word 'crisis' as a negative term, but most people would also recognise events like leaving home, getting married, having a baby, even going on holiday, as having some of the elements of crisis. According to the Collins English Dictionary (1995) the word crisis comes from the Greek word 'krisis', meaning decision, challenge or opportunity. We seem to be more receptive to change at such times because we struggle to maintain our balance, our adrenalin perhaps flows more freely, and we are capable of all sorts of efforts we could not normally make: for example the person who is afraid of flying who takes the aeroplane to Australia to visit his sick brother.

It is this receptivity which is very helpful to you and your reluctant client at a crisis point in the latter's life. Obviously the event itself could be any one of a number of horrible things: being diagnosed with a life threatening illness, going to prison, the death of someone dear, even having you imposed upon them!

In order to cope, your client tries to fall back on whatever he/she has done before when threatened. These 'strategies' vary from the very helpful, such as finding out lots of information about the situation he/she is in, to the more unhelpful like drink or illegal drugs. If there is someone like you around after the crisis, the client is more likely to use this chance of a sounding board, rather than rush into unconstructive action because of the degree of distress or fear surrounding her/him.

Supposing you have learned a few tried and tested ways of responding to your client, you have a much better chance of using the crisis to its full potential for him/her to cope better

with life generally. I, along with Nigel Horner, an inspired social work teacher, devised the following list of useful tips from our reading and experience:

1. Give the client as much information as you can.

This could include finding out about particular conditions or illnesses, arranging for your client to see other professionals, or making visits to care homes. It is really important not to withhold difficult information, unless the client, the needs of others, or his/her condition really does preclude this. You will always be imparting problem information in conjunction with, or in the presence of other professionals.

2. Use pictures, leaflets, the web and other aids to communication.

Information makes more sense if it can be referred to again and again, as the person may be too shocked to take it in at first.

3. Try to enlist the support of others, such as family, a team or a network.

Many family reconciliations take place as a result of crisis, and perhaps for the first time, your client may actually gain comfort from association with people who have similar problems.

4. Ask the person what has helped before when they have been in crisis.

This is an important point, as we often assume others have the same strategies as ourselves. For example, I remember a clergyman who simply could not understand why a newly bereaved person he was visiting would prefer to watch her favourite soap rather than talk to him.

5. Allow plenty of time for people in shock.

As you may know from your own experience, people in shock often cannot accomplish the simplest task or take in a single word.

6. Stay with the pain.

Physically, this means choosing the setting which will be most comforting for the service user, not yourself. An example which springs to mind was when a young service user insisted on asking me very sensitive questions in the crowded waiting room of a court. The noise and hubbub, combined with the crisis of court attendance, helped the young man to feel less naked in his discomfort.

7. Acknowledge that this is a terrible situation, quite irresolvable.

This is suitable in very negative situations, where the same type of crisis has occurred over and over again. You will need to feel confident in using this approach, but the following example may ring some bells for you:
Sophie has run away from her children's home for the eighth time. You suggest to Sophie and the staff team that there is no point in discussing ways to help Sophie to stay as she obviously hates the home and everyone in it. You then ensure that Sophie has the chance to speak first.

8. Make an agreement about who is going to do what.

A crisis is a situation where the service user might actually be glad for someone to help out, without taking over completely. For example, a helper could contact family or other professionals, arrange transport or make a cup of tea.

(Substantially Horner and Kindred 1997, pp 26-27).

At risk of stating the obvious - matters are often described as crises when they are actually your problems, not things which disturb the client's balance in the way described above. It may well be essential that your client agrees to allow you to have access to his/her finances, but you may have to wait for this information till there is some urgency for the client. I remember one person who needed to be at the point of being evicted from her flat before she could cope with supplying the details which made eviction improbable.

Finally, crisis was described above as a *dangerous* opportunity. The potential is always there for the involuntary client to miss this particular chance by refusing to take medication, running away, being unable to let anyone near his/her pain. Of course some people go to pieces and never recover from a crisis. My father lost his wife early in their marriage, and his life thereafter was a kind of grey monochrome. Just supposing a skilled helper had been at hand to help, I believe the outcome could have been very different.

Some people show their feelings...

...not you, of course!

This part is about one of the paradoxes mentioned in the introduction. If we do not like someone, I believe that it is not as easy to disguise this as we think, however many hours of training we have had, or how high our level of self discipline. Involuntary clients are like children (both having little power) in the uncanny sense they have of gauging how you actually feel, rather than how you present yourself. So how can this be managed, since you cannot possibly feel positive all the time?

Firstly we can control our actions, ie not letting our dislike of someone translate into punishing them. This is easier said than done: having someone trustworthy to talk to about such situations is essential. Secondly we can be tactfully honest: if someone is not allowing you to get a word in, or insidiously making sexual overtures, it is much better to say that 'it is difficult to go on while...', or whatever form of words is comfortable for you, than to let the situation run on. It is hard to put this into practice, especially with someone who does not really want you. Be comforted by research which shows that involuntary clients did much better when their workers were honest about their behaviour: not to be so was seen as subtly condoning anti-social actions (Andrews and Bonta 1990). These experts also found that detrimental comments in files about clients tended to be related to the latter's progress. It is as if words like 'lazy', 'manipulative' come over the airwaves from your office to your client as surely as if you had shouted them through a loudspeaker.

I believe that we cannot help our feelings. Also the pressures of life and work on any particular day can be too much - but we have to meet our obligations somehow. Training *does* help. Try the following, from McDermott and O'Connor (1996, pp 42-43), before you meet the client:

To have more choice about your emotional state, identify what sights, sounds, tastes, smells and touches put you in an unhelpful or negative state? Irritation, hostility, depression, feeling helpless, harassed or fearful are examples of unhelpful state. Sad states are not necessarily unhelpful. Is your trigger a particular tone of voice? A particular facial expression? The sound of rain first thing in the morning? A full in-tray?

When you notice the trigger, you have taken a significant step towards breaking its hold. Start by pacing yourself. Pay attention to how you feel. 'Do I need to feel this way?' 'Do I want to feel this way?'

When you find yourself in an unhelpful state, simply stay with it in an interested way. Pace yourself. Notice which parts of your body are involved in it and which are not. Being with the state in this way can cause it to change and evolve. You may feel tired and feel like relaxing for a few minutes. You may feel renewed energy. Your state will change once you give it attention. States organise your physiology in a characteristic way. Changing physiology changes state. This may be why pretending to be happy can actually have real physical effects. Changing thinking will not work unless it brings a shift in physiology - whether deliberate or involuntary is irrelevant.

Food for thought!

..true or false?

This is another of the things which professionals rarely agree about. I thought it was worth looking at what some experts have said about this subject, particularly where reluctant clients are concerned.

Your client does not want you, so you are doing your best to find a genuine point of contact. What could be more natural than to talk about your own problems as a parent with someone who is being closely supervised, or may have had his/her children placed with foster parents? You may be aching to tell your client, who is finding it difficult to manage household tasks, about your father, who felt just the same about losing independence, and who now loves the services he receives.

On the other hand, you may have taken to heart some of the earlier remarks in this book about informality and personal safety, or have been told that it is always wrong to speak about any of your own experiences, or those of family and friends, to clients because their situation is always different, and even if it isn't, they will never be comforted by the connection.

The case for sharing your own feelings a little, and giving such information as whether or not you have children, if asked, was generally thought to be friendly and helpful by involuntary clients. But a group of experts, Hepworth et al (1997), having consulted much research, concluded that results were equally divided for and against giving information about yourself. There is not a single view!

So perhaps it is helpful to keep in mind a few questions:

- who is going to benefit from me talking about myself ?

- am I actually wasting precious time by talking about me?

- am I avoiding tackling difficult issues?

- do I want to be liked?

- am I simply tired and hungry and want to go home?

It is also quite feasible to mention experiences as though they are not personal, if you think these could be helpful, eg ' I once heard of someone who hated the personal care service; he now gives talks on it to groups of new service users'. Films and videos come into the category of introducing subjects in a less personal, but interesting way (bearing in mind the cautionary note under Staying Safe).

However the starting point for this topic was your desire to find a point of contact. Rather than speaking about yourself, try the following, which has been contributed by Cath Kindred:

1. Select a particular day to do this exercise when you are going to see as many people as possible, either clients or colleagues.

2. On the chosen day, carry a small notebook with you.

3. During your contact with each person or group, note the number of times you hear a particular word or phrase. For example: 'money' might be a popular one!

This simple exercise gives you a more accurate clue about what is really uppermost in people's minds than asking them questions. You can then use this knowledge to make sure the subjects which you have heard over and over are discussed or dealt with in some other way. Caution: I acknowledge that you may be very tired of hearing certain subjects! These may actually obscure the ones you need to hear - the casually 'dropped in' words.

Square pegs don't usually fit in round holes...

... sometimes helpers try very hard to make them

This does not mean there is anything wrong with either the pegs or the holes - just that they don't fit! In our work with people, we may not fit very well for all sorts of reasons, some of which may not be so obvious.

At risk of being seen as negative, I have decided to start with things which don't work, as I think this will help in preparing the ground for looking at what can and may work, and because in my experience these things are used so often that they add to the common perception of reluctant clients as 'difficult if not impossible'.

We often *think* we are operating gently, but our language is less than helpful: 'We have had a report that you are harming your children' is not a good beginning. You may feel that this is an extreme example - no one would start like that – but not only has the author heard something like it many times, but these words are a direct quotation from the research of David Gough (1993, p. 8). He also says that European child protection workers are much better than British ones at the introduction of sensitive topics!

Then there are the 'methods' which don't work, the 'square pegs'. We still seem to hold on to the remnants of psychoanalysis, from which social work methods partially evolved. Clients who do not want you are likely to talk about their past when they want to, rather than as part of a structured interview. I have found, like Geraldine McDonald (2001) that trying to help such clients to develop insight and make links with the present is rarely helpful - they will gain far more from the humane way you treat them.

It follows that trying to help your client understand by explanation why his/her way of life does not work is likely to fail (Trotter 1996, in Keats 1999).

Setting goals only works if the client is truly committed to them, in other words there must be 'something in it' for her/him.

If the individual client is always seen as the problem, rather than the family or society also contributing, poor results are likely to ensue. I have also found that formal therapeutic games or exercises rarely work with individuals – except for ordinary board and card games, which clients can see as normal.

There are always exceptions, and I would not wish to appear to denigrate methods which I have enjoyably and productively used with many clients. I have found inspiration in Chris Trotter's books, referred to earlier. Try *Working with involuntary clients (2006).*

It has also been discovered that workers found it very difficult in practice to change their conventional ways of operating (Gough 1993). We imagine, for example, that we convey what we mean. So it may be helpful to switch the focus back to ourselves for an exercise on the vital skill of making things clearer for others. Try this in your staff team:

*Explain to the group that one person is going to start by making a statement beginning with 'I think/feel/would like', for example 'I wish I could get out of here'. All statements must begin with 'I'. The person on his/her left will then say something which she/he thinks is helpful, for example 'Do you mean you would like to see your family'? All responses must begin with 'Do you mean'? The first speaker must respond by only a 'yes' or a 'no' depending on whether the second speaker has got it right or not. If a 'no', the person to the left of the second speaker will try another reply, for example 'Do you mean you feel uncomfortable'. This will continue by moving to the person on the left until a 'yes' has been achieved. If no 'yes' is achieved, the original speaker will be asked what response he/she would have liked. There must be no discussion or argument! The exercise progresses until everyone has had a turn to make their own statement beginning with 'I'. Only then allow discussion about what has been experienced.

It is surprising what comes from a very simple exercise. The game format can make people much less self-conscious - and hopefully more so - in a positive way! Participants have to try to put their own agendas into words, and listen to someone else's at the same time, exactly as we do in our work.

As a footnote, it is interesting that it was learned relatively early in therapeutic work that some of the 'common sense' methods of helping did not work, even with psycho-analytic clients, who presumably were highly motivated: *'The psychologist has come to see that nothing is achieved by telling, persuading, admonishing, giving good advice'* (Jung).

Now: move on to what does seem to work!

*Substantially reproduced, by permission, from © ***Once upon a group exercises***
Southwell: 4M Publications

You may find that your client is far more interested in the cup of tea served at the group meeting than the subject ...

... in fact the cup of tea could be more important

The particular challenge of working with people who don't want you is finding ways of operating on an ordinary human level.

This sounds pitifully obvious, but in fact many books about theory are concerned with methods which are primarily designed for clients who have chosen to accept help, as

previously discussed. I have found that a different range of theory is important for the unwilling client.

Maslow, a humanistic writer of the 1970s, set out a 'hierarchy of human needs' which govern our existence:

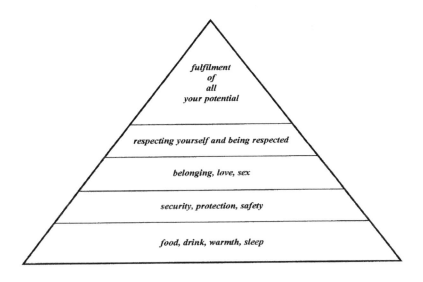

If as helpers we give the 'obvious' two bottom layers a second look, we may find a useful clue for 'methods' to use with involuntary clients. The particularly pertinent thing which Maslow seemed to emphasise was that the higher needs *cannot* be met until the basic ones have been satisfied. It is true that there have always been men and women who have triumphed over atrocious physical conditions and performed quite staggering feats of heroism or self-education: in my view it is wrong to compare these with anyone else's struggle, which may be, for him/her, just to get through the day. Most people cannot rise to the heights unless they are fed, warm and feel safe.

I remember watching a particularly gifted student working: the latter did not ask her client a single question; simply commented on what she noticed: for example the temperature of the room, the fact that her client looked tired, the ingredients for a meal on the table. In a relaxed interview she had achieved a remarkably full assessment of her quite seriously mentally ill woman's current mood, physical state, and needs.

The use of humour is mentioned by several experts as being useful with involuntary clients. For example, Lawrence Schulman (1991) found that child protection workers who had a sense of humour were more likely to be viewed by their clients as helpful, skilful and trustworthy. Later another two experts Pollio (1995), and Struthers (1999), who both worked in the statutory sector, tell of situations where humour which is directly related to the situation in hand can be very helpful in taking the heat out of things. Both writers caution against telling jokes, and discourage anything which could be demeaning to the client. I am sure you will have direct experience of all these kinds of humour from your schooldays, when you were yourself an involuntary client! Certainly I have always found myself on safest ground when I use humour against myself. For example, a young client once told me he would like to see X. I replied that sounded a good idea, what about inviting him to tea? It quickly transpired that X was a well-known pop star. This gaffe, which the young person never allowed me to forget, forged a new bond between us.

The nearest I would come to formal activities with reluctant clients is the 'life story book'. This is a creative, sometimes fun, often emotional, way to help clients remember, reflect, and move on from previous parts of their lives. The idea came originally from children's workers who wished to help young clients who could not remember their past, but it can be equally useful for adults with mental health problems and older people whose present seems somewhat empty. Most people are intrigued as long as they know you have no ulterior motive.

Life story books

There is no particular formula. The basics are: a scrapbook and some guaranteed time over a few weeks.

Explain that a lot of people find it helpful to make a book about their life, which is personal to them, and may help to bring out all sorts of talents and interests which have never been discovered or been hidden.

You do not have to start with the past. Many of the clients we are talking abut are likely to wish to forget this. Begin with photographs. If the client does not possess any, now is an excellent time to acquire some!

Give time for the client to talk about whatever the photographs recall for him/her. Do not avoid painful recollections; these are helpful so long as it is the client, not the worker who decides to speak about them.

Mementos, letters, things the client wants to write, draw or paint are all very useful.

If at all possible, encourage the client to include material about good times, however insignificant these may seem. Obviously these must be real for the client; a 'count your blessings' exercise simply is not on.

Finally, you and the client should let family (if appropriate from a confidentiality point of view), or carers know that you are doing this work together, so that maximum support can be given.

Ways of successful working, then, centre round simple things, shopping, homemaking, clothes, helping your client to feel as safe as possible in his/ her environment, and 'life'.

There are many ways of saying thank you...

...which do you accept?

The giving of presents is another topic which is very controversial, possibly more so where reluctant clients are concerned. A starting point may be that many of us are much happier with giving than receiving in life generally. If so, it is worth wondering why this is.

In order to unpick the issue a little more, imagine that an involuntary client has a small gift-wrapped parcel in his/her hand which is being offered to you. Imagine you can stop the clock for a while and ask yourself the following questions:

- what are my feelings about his/her gesture?

It is really important to answer this one first, as your feelings may sway your judgement in the wrong direction. The range of feelings goes from pleased and touched through to wary and angry.

- why does the client want to give me something?

If you are worried that there may be an element of bribe you will obviously refuse as gently and firmly as possible. If you have been working together well, there could be a genuine desire to thank you. It simply does not occur to some people that presents can be seen as bribes.

- does the organisation I work with have rules about receiving presents?

If you are not allowed to accept presents your decision is made for you. Having said that, I feel that there are times when a small gift should be accepted, with the explanation that you will need to pass on the present to your boss so that it is shared by others. If you do accept anything, it must always be recorded in your official notes.

There are a lot of 'it depends' yet to be covered:

- obviously expensive presents and legacies are absolutely out.

- is the present a coded (or not so coded!) message? One new student found it difficult to see that a gift of six pairs of tights from a man to her, a young woman, may not have been a wise acquisition.

- it is lovely to accept a drink (non alcoholic) which someone has made for you.

- a client who was obviously wealthy, took it in turns with the author to buy the drinks when their meetings took place in a coffee bar - this was important in bringing an aspect of equality to the working relationship.

Whatever your conclusions generally, experience does seem to suggest that you consult each client's records well before presents become an issue as there are safety issues to be considered in addition to all the above. There is only a very small minority of people who would deliberately try to poison you, but it is not worth being the target for hatred which is most certainly meant for someone else.

This applies to drinks which could be laced with something. I remember a colleague being given a cake of the 'hash' variety. We all vary in our tolerance of cups which are not washed as well as we should like - remember you are a helper not a martyr. Having said this, I cannot remember a single instance of being ill from any of the 500 or so drinks I have consumed in clients' homes.

Working on your own or with others, decide which of the following you would accept:

- *a cup of tea from someone who is schizophrenic*

- *an inexpensive bunch of flowers from a couple whom you are helping to adopt a baby*

- *a lift in a client's car*

- *a small box of chocolates from someone on probation*

- *a bag of sweets from an eight year old which he tells you he has bought with his own pocket money*

- *flowers from relatives of a terminally ill person whom you have helped to place in a hospice*

No doubt you will feel that all these come into the 'it depends' category, but the author cannot resist making a few comments on them!

Contrary to popular belief, schizophrenia does not automatically make someone dangerous, merely tormented and unhappy. You need to be aware of the client's history, usual behaviour and mental state at the time you visit. These factors are almost always as important as the medical diagnosis for judging safety.

Adoption rules state that 'no gifts of cash or kind'may be offered by applicants. I remember being very embarrassed at handing back the couple's gift, as they were both sincere, completely unaware of the implications, just tearful and grateful. Having taken advice, I suggested that a cup of coffee at the adopters' expense would be lovely after the final court hearing.

Accepting lifts would be highly questionable from both a safety and ethical point of view.

Taking a box of chocolates is definitely in the 'it depends' category. If you are the person writing a report for court on which the client's future depends, this is very different from being a non-statutory carer.

Children are heart-warming in their generosity and it would seem churlish to refuse the present. However you do need to think about the context. If the child's parent is your involuntary client, proceed with extreme caution, since your acceptance could later be used against you. On the other hand a gift from a child who does not live in his/her own home, and to whom you are a significant adult, is another matter altogether.

The flowers from grateful relatives are also a third party gift, but acceptance is much less problematic, in my opinion. It can ease pain a little to give something to a helper, however much the latter feels she/he was 'only doing her/his job'.

To sum up: if in doubt - don't!

What you sow tends to be what you reap...

...though you won't see the harvest

There is nothing remarkable about the fact that someone who is not committed to his/her clients is not likely to have good results or experience much satisfaction, whereas the worker who enjoys the work will communicate the fact that he/she feels positive and believes the best of people - this is not the same as being unrealistic. A psychiatric colleague of mine once said she thought that social workers' expectations of clients were generally too high - there is food for thought here - even though it may not be clear whether the psychiatrist was implying that her own professional body had lower sights!

As with all work of this sort, some kind of evaluation is useful. However, we are unlikely to elicit thanks or much acknowledgement that the time together has been helpful. Over the years you may find a consistency about what clients say which is extremely valuable, if not always comfortable! For example many clients have told me that they valued my being honest with them. This inspires one of the key themes of this book.

I should like to make it clear at this point that many involuntary clients are very appreciative of our services. The case that they are not has been overstated in order to highlight the fact that we cannot *expect* gratitude.

However the real rewards of working with people who did not want you are the things you learn about yourself and the world. Because such clients are not always so concerned with some of the social niceties as more 'motivated' people may be, they cut through your 'methods', 'assessments', 'goals', and other strategies like the proverbial knife through butter. I remember working with a student colleague during a shopping trip with a client. The latter had planned carefully and well where to shop, what the client needed, how to ensure the trip wasn't too tiring - the client was somewhat infirm. Money was available so that the client was not out of pocket. As the little group, client, student and I, progressed along the supermarket aisles, the client began to look more and more confused. Eventually I asked him what was wrong. He told me he didn't know what 'toiletries' were; the shopping list had in fact been made by the staff of the residential home in which he lived. Some people, and certainly not men of 80 years old, in the poor area of the big city where the client grew up, did not buy toiletries. So all the student's hard work seemed pointless - trying to work as a team with other professionals leads us along all sorts of by-ways. I hope the student concerned, if he should read this, does not mind being cited. I do not know how to contact him, and the wrong assumptions were not his fault, simply a case of care staff trying to bring some extra comfort into someone's life.

As far as involuntary clients are concerned, we may never see

the results of our efforts. Very occasionally you will hear news of someone years later, or learn that a difficult and unpopular decision you took has turned out well. One such magical example: a small baby of African/Caribbean heritage was placed with a white foster mother in a very white area. There were all sorts of reservations about the placement, but the foster mother loved the little girl so much; her physical and emotional care of the child was excellent, and her support for the birth mother so genuine, that she was eventually allowed to adopt her. Some thirty years later a quality newspaper did a series on adoption, and my day was made one Saturday by reading a testimonial, which from description and photo was unmistakably the 'baby' speaking about her adoptive mother and the wonderful childhood she had experienced. Note: I still believe that it is much better to place children with foster/adoptive parents of the same race as their own, if possible.

Mostly you will find satisfaction in having worked as well as you could with another human being, even becoming very fond of him/her. I enjoy gardening, which is why the analogy of very small seeds turning into beautiful flowers means so much to me. Sometimes you will hear of a client's life turning to tragedy - these are fortunately few.

This book has been less about *how* to work with people and much more about *what* is important while doing so. It is not about results, even though these may creep up on you unexpectedly like the flowers. There are few definite endings:

'The world is round and the place which may seem like the end may also be the beginning' Ivy Baker Priest (1958).

References

Andrews, D., Bonta J., 1998. *The psychology of criminal conduct.* Cincinnati: Anderson.

Baker Priest, I., 1958. *Parade.* New York: Parade.

BBC World Service, undated. *Teaching English.* London: British Council

Cryer, J., 1990. *Games people play in educational games, simulations and workshops: a transactional analysis perspective.* Simulation games for learning, 1990, 20 (4), 368-377.

Curtin, C., 2006. Untitled. Australia: *www.curtin.edu.au/online/netiquette.btml:*

Egan, G., 1994. *The skilled helper.* USA: Brooks/Cole.

Goldsmith, M., 1996. *Hearing the voice of people with dementia.* London: Jessica Kingsley.

Hepworth, D., Rooney, R., and Larson, J., 1997. *Direct social work practice: theory and skills.* Pacific Grove: Cole.

Hoffman, L., 1993. *Exchanging voices: a collaborative approach to family therapy.* London: Karnac.

Horner, N., and Kindred, M., 1997. *Using crisis intervention and task-centred theories in social work.* Birmingham: Open learning Foundation.

Howe, D., 1990. *The client's view in context.* In: Social work and social welfare yearbook, Eds: P. Carter, T. Jeffs, M. Smith. Milton Keynes: OUP.

Keats, D., 2000. *Interviewing: a practical guide for students and professionals.* Buckingham: OUP.

Kindred, M., and Kindred, M., 2000. *Once upon a group exercises.* Southwell: 4M Publications.

Kirk, S., Koeske, G., and Koeske, R., 1993. *Changes in health and job attitudes of case managers providing intensive services.* Washington: American Psychiatric Association

Malpass, R., 1996. *Face recognition at the interface of psychology, law and medicine* In: H. Grad et al., Key issues in cross cultural psychology. Lisse: Swets and Zeitlinger 7-21.

Maslow, A., 1970. *Motivation and personality.* New York: Harper and Row.

May, R., 1972 *Power and innocence.* Norton: New York.

McDermott, T., and O'Connor, J., 1996. *Neuro-linguistic programming and health.* London: Thorsons.

Mehrabian, A., 1972. *Non-verbal communication.* Chicago: Aldine Atherton.

Miller, J., 1996. *Social care practice.* London: Hodder Education.

Miller, W., and Rollnick, S., 2004. *Motivational interviewing.* New York: Guildford.

Pollio, D., 1995. *Use of humour in crisis intervention.* Families in society: the journal of contemporary human services, 76(6), 376-384.

Ritts, V., and Stein, J., undated. *Six ways to improve your non-verbal communications.* Edwardsville: Illinois University.

Seligman, M., 1995. *Learned optimism.*   New York: Free Press.

Schulman, L., 1991. *Co-ordination and child protection.* Edinburgh: HMSO.

Struthers, J., 1999. *An investigation into community psychiatric nurses' use of humour during client interactions.* Journal of advanced nursing, 29(5), 1197-1204.

Usiskin, J., 1998. *Working with disability.*   Ely: Fenman.